Thomas M Goodman, Harry A. Houston

A Thrilling Record

Founded on facts and observations obtained during ten days' experience

with Colonel William T. Anderson

Thomas M Goodman, Harry A. Houston

A Thrilling Record
*Founded on facts and observations obtained during ten days' experience with
Colonel William T. Anderson*

ISBN/EAN: 9783337343859

Printed in Europe, USA, Canada, Australia, Japan

Cover: Foto ©Andreas Hilbeck / pixelio.de

More available books at **www.hansebooks.com**

A THRILLING RECORD:

FOUNDED ON FACTS AND OBSERVATIONS OBTAINED DURING TEN
DAYS' EXPERIENCE WITH

COLONEL WILLIAM T. ANDERSON,

(THE NOTORIOUS GUERRILLA CHIEFTAIN,)

BY

SERGEANT THOS. M. GOODMAN,

The only survivor of the inhuman massacre at Centralia, Mo.,
September 27, 1864; and an eye-witness of the brutal
and barbarous treatment by the guerrillas of
the dead, wounded, and captured
of Major Johnson's
command.

———

EDITED AND PREPARED FOR THE PRESS BY
CAPT. HARRY A. HOUSTON.

———— • ————

DES MOINES, IOWA:
MILLS & CO., STEAM BOOK & JOB PRINTING HOUSE.
1868.

PREFACE.

It is somewhat remarkable that an event should have transpired during the late rebellion, so replete with horror and atrocious deeds as the massacre of Centralia, and at this late day still have failed to secure a place in history. Perhaps the very enormity of the crimes perpetrated there, have tended to *silence in awe* the pen of the historian ; else, the doubt and uncertainty attached to the written and oral statements made heretofore concerning it, have induced the fear on their part, that its introduction into their written histories might affect the authenticity of the whole. From some cause, there exists to-day no published history of the affair, and it is partly to supply this deficiency, and to fulfill a promise made in years by-gone, that this little volume is given to the world.

The massacre at Centralia has had but few, if any parallels in the history of the world, and we offer no excuse in reproducing these ''scenes infernal,'' further than a desire to do justice to all concerned—friends and foes.

The facts and incidents related in this volume are from unquestioned authority —the lips of a participant, and eye-witness to all its horrors, and the *only survivor* of the occasion. His relation was simple, concise, yet particular, and can not fail to leave a conviction of its *truth* upon the mind of the reader. One of the most interesting features of this volume consists in the preciseness and distinctness with which the narrator, Mr. Goodman, has recalled and described the peculiarities of guerrilla life in the bush—ten days of which he experienced while a prisoner in the hands of the band responsible for the murder of the '' Boys in Blue '' who fell at Centralia. The portrait, '' drawn from memory,'' of the appearance of the guerrilla leader, must be of interest to all who have long felt the name of WILLIAM T. ANDERSON, the guerrilla, as being synonomous with every horrible crime that '' war's dread field '' might cruelly sanction.

We feel that it would be but a task of supererogation to commend this volume to the comrades-in-arms, who, for years of ''bloody strife and 'mid war's alarms,'' stood shoulder to shoulder in the service with Mr. Goodman ; and we but make this brief note to remind them that '' TOM,'' now as then, ''will always be as good as his word,'' and herein fulfills the promise he made to you.

H. A. HOUSTON, *Editor.*

CERTIFICATE.

HAWLEYVILLE, Page Co., Iowa,
August, 1868.

This is to certify that we are personally known to Sergt. Thos. Goodman, and the fact of his capture and escape from Anderson's notorious guerrillas, and feel justified in recommending his statements as fully entitled to the credence of the public.

G. H. RUMBAUGH, P. M., Hawleyville.
WM. L. STONE, Merchant, "
CAPT. JOHN WHITCOMB, Clarinda,

A TRUE NARRATIVE.

CHAPTER I.

Explanatory and Introductory.

To write a book, was the last possible task we should have
ever expected to be employed at, nevertheless, like some of
the famous "undertakengs" of the renowned Col. Crocket, it
may possibly "*e'nd better nor it begun*," or in the same manner,
as some of that marvellous hero's encounters with the wild
habitants of the woods, "lucky." Without unnecessary delay
or further apology, we therefore assume the task, and we can
possibly conceive of no more fitting introduction of our
hero than is given by the *gist* of the following letter from
the Rev. Mr. Striker, a Presbyterian clergyman, penned
shortly after the passage of the particular events to which he
alludes in his closing illustration. The position he assumes is
worthy of reflection; and it does certainly appear, as a *special
act* of Providence, that in the face of all precedent established
by Anderson's notorious guerillas, the life of Mr. Goodman
should have been spared, while *twenty six* of his comrades,
equally entitled with himself to the claims of mercy, should
have been shot down in cold blood before his eyes. The sub-
joined *extract* renders its own explanation, and we cheerfully
indorse it as a fitting preface to the narrator's own experience:

"There are few persons, perhaps, who enjoy better opportunities of observing the workings of Divine Providence than our western missionaries who live on the frontier, and are fed and clothed by miracle, as "Elijah was fed and clothed by the ravens," or, as the "garments of the children of Israel waxed not old." But the instance I am about to relate is of a different type to the class alluded to above. It is a providence which illustrates that precious promise of Christ recorded in Math. x : 42 : "Whosoever shall give to drink unto these little ones a cup of cold water only, in the name of a disciple, *verily* I say unto you, *he* shall not lose his reward."

"About two years ago there was a man in my little congregation at Hawleyville, Iowa, who was not much in the habit of attending church, but had on that day taken his seat among the hearers in a newly-erected school-house, and seemed to be an attentive hearer, and was, perhaps, somewhat affected by the discourse. After service he turned to one of the members and remarked :

"'I understand that you pay rent for the use of this building ?'

"'Yes,' was the reply.

"'How much do you pay ?' continued he.

"'Well, not very much,' replied the member, 'perhaps a dollar a month.'

"'Well,' said the man 'I will pay half that rent.'

The offer was thankfully accepted. Shortly after, Mr. Thomas Goodman (for that was the name of the man), enlisted in the service of his country, and the officers of the church supposed that probably he had forgotten his promise, but when they came to settle the rent, they found one-half of it paid, and credited to the account of the little church. Here is one side of the picture. Time elapsed ; years rolled by. Mr. Goodman had probably forgotten this little act of kindness to the Lord's poor people, but the blessed Saviour had treasured it up in his memory, and had determined to *reward* it; for he says, 'whosoever, not merely of his own people, but *whomsoever.*'

"A few weeks ago that notorious guerrilla chief, Bill Anderson, captured some twenty-seven soldiers returning to their homes and families, all buoyant with the hope of joining loved ones in a short time. The train was stopped at Centralia, set on fire, and the soldiers ordered out in line to be shot. Mr. Goodman was one of those soldiers. Entreaties and assurances of the doomed men availed nothing; hope had departed; all prepared for death. How now, blessed Saviour, wilt Thou fulfill thy promise? Wait one moment, and see. A thought flashes over the mind of Anderson: 'I have lost a sergeant; perhaps there is one here that I may exchange for my own; or if mine is killed, then will I glut my vengeance on this federal sergeant.' Accordingly he gives the order:

"'If there is a sergeant in this line, let him step out of the ranks!'"

Mr. Goodman steps aside, is put under guard, and his companions were shot down like beasts.

The names of these victims of guerrilla outrage reached their mourning relatives, and Mr. Goodman's name is recorded among the victims. The benign Redeemer grants to his wife also, a ray of hope in the midst of the bitterness of her affliction. She dreamed that she saw her husband; met him returning home; she waked—it was only a dream. She dreamed again the same dream, and in the morning she set out to meet her husband; and just where she beheld him in her dream, she met him! Mr. Goodman did not lose his reward; his *life is given him as his reward!* Infidels, I know may query, 'How do you know what motives influence the mind of the Almighty in the ordering of events like this? We answer, that doubtless one motive is a regard for his own promise; and here is the promise—here the fulfillment, made manifest.

"The facts I have related, are notorious all through Northwestern Missouri about the capture of the train at Centralia, the massacre of the soldiers—Mr G. alone, being the exception. The escape of Mr. Goodman is also well known; and as the *only man living* of the "doomed and fatal line" formed; by Anderson's order on that memorable occasion, it is to be hoped that some day the public will receive a correct and detailed version of the horrible affair, from Mr. Goodman's own pen."—*Cor. Presbyterian.*

CHAPTER II.

Reader, it seems strange that I should be this day engaged,
as I am, in rehearsing scenes through which I once passed—
more like one in a dream, perhaps, than as an author—seeking
for material from which to indite a book. That I became a
party to what I shall attempt to describe, of my own free
will, you will doubtless readily deny, when you have closed
the volume which I hope to lay before you, complete in its
details of the most monstrous and inhuman atrocities ever
perpetrated by beings wearing the form of man. I certainly
should not have attempted even this plain statement of facts
occurring under my own eye, did I for one moment believe
the effort would be criticised and ridicule, perhaps, laid upon
my simple description of persons, places and events. Perhaps, as the only survivor of the original twenty-seven,
placed by the arch-fiend Anderson in that fated line from
which twenty-six brave, loyal hearts, bid an eternal farewell
to earth—perhaps, I say, I might reasonably claim the right
to become the historian of the event; and yet, that fact alone
has heretofore, in a measure, deterred me from assuming such
responsibility. I revere the memory of my fallen comrades
too dearly to rejoice in the fortune that leaves me, the only
living man, bound by the most sacred of all associations, to

do honor and justice to my fallen comrades; for aye, ten thousand of the highest eulogies ever penned, would not repay me for all I must soon again endure, even in fancy, as I recall in these sketches the horrible scenes of blood and brutality I was compelled to witness. History should prove a faithful expounder of events as they occur—never the *apologist* for their occurrence. No written account that has as yet met my eye, has ever given a full, detailed, accurate account of the massacre occurring at Centralia. I have read many that were penned by civilians, who were witnesses of the execution of those defenseless soldiers; and again others undoubtedly written by some venal scribbler, and penned for dollars and cents, seeking only to satisfy the expectant greed of an eager public; and yet, in not one of those has justice even been meted to the dead, or accorded to the living of the great number on both sides who were participants in that horrible massacre. Men, professedly Union and loyal men, descended from the throne of truth, and by garbled sentences and misquoted statements sought to cover up or conceal the iniquities of parties interested. My purpose is to give "a plain unvarnished tale," noting and speaking only of such facts as came directly under my own observation, or that were imparted to me by unquestioned authority.

Kind reader, I hope no one who peruses this narrative will impute other than the best motives to me, nor accuse me of seeking vain glory for name or deeds in inditing this simple record for posterity. I hope and I pray sincerely, that the revelations it contains—unmasking as it does the "man divine," and exhibiting the "inherent demon" in his soul—may live long in the memory of the general reader as a "warning note," bidding him, through all time to come, to war with all the strength of his manhood against any principle involving an hereditary power of one human being over another. To my

children, then, if to none other, this record will prove of
value, inasmuch as its perusal will ever prove a reminder to
them of what their father suffered in securing to them a
continuance of the great blessings of civil and religious
liberty, either of which were incompatible to the purposes
and designs of traitors. These *are* and of a *right* should ever
continue the birth-right of every child born on American
soil, and we again bequeath them to posterity, re-baptized in
the sufferings and blood of every soldier who fell a martyr in
the Union cause. And now, having said so much by way of
an apology for entering the "charmed circle of authorship,"
I shall proceed, as connectedly as the passage of the events
will admit, with my narrative.

Ten days following the capture of Atlanta, Ga., and its oc-
cupation by the federal forces, myself and some twenty others
were made glad by the reception of our long-promised and
eagerly-expected furloughs. I have often wondered if the
word *furlough* gave the faintest possible idea to the mind of
a civilian of *all* that it expressed to a soldier's heart and ear !
Is it possible that our wordly-wise, toiling patriots who
stayed at home "smelling the battle from afar" and satisfying
their *natural pride* of country by the praises bestowed upon
her brave defenders,—I say, I have often wondered if such
men knew what a fourlough meant; or was it possible that
they could ? I honestly believe not.

With the furlough came the "doffing of war's insignia"—
the bidding adieu to all its "pomp and circumstance"—and
the partings, not tender or in hurried whispers, but bluff and
hale, and hopeful—prototyping the feeling tugging at the
honest soldier's heart. Then came our last and most solemn
ceremony—parting with the cook. Singing the following
stanza, as a parting salute to his many virtues, one by one
we sadly bade him adieu:

A few may bless, and many curse,
And dream, ere they awaken,
Of home, where hogs are made with *hams*,
And not all " rusty bacon ! "
Then let us faith and courage have,
The " signs " can't be mistaken—
We soon shall bid adieu to thee,
" Hard-tack " and "rusty bacon."

One loud huzza, and tramp, tramp, tramp, in quick time, with eager hearts we moved to the station and got aboard the train which was to bear us homeward. No anticipations so sweet as ours! No dream so cherished as the strange and playful tender fancies of those few brief hours—those *first* hours of a soldier's release from the line of duty and discipline. Memory, ever faithful to our tenderest loves, turns backward to our subject of greatest solicitude, and home, our dear old home, once more looms up before us. We are there in fancy; we almost feel and return the warmth of the first kind, hand-pressure of welcoming friends. The loved are there to meet us, and as we pause in the midst of these fancies, lest they have too rapid an ending, and the illusion vanish, we almost *feel* tender, soft arms about our neck, and hear an infant voice prattling in our ear. These dreams are the oases in the life of a soldier, and never a blue-coat can you show me, but knows what it is to dream like this. Each has his particular fancy, and such fancies furnish the "*dessert*" to hard-tack and bacon.

We left Atlanta on the 22d day of September, 1864. At Big Shanty, thirty-five miles from Atlanta, we found the track torn up, thus necessitating the stoppage of our train. Wheeler's (rebel) cavalry had made a sudden dash, surprised the guard, and destroyed some eighty rods or more of the line before they were driven off by a re-inforcement sent from the guard-station above. Luckily many of us belonged to the

First Missouri Engineer Regiment, and had experience in railroad construction. We all therefore worked with a will and zeal never to be obtained from a soldier only in emergencies like this, and in the course of some four or five hours, all was declared properly completed, and with loud cheers we bid adieu to the scene of Wheeler's exploit. We arrived at Chattanooga in safety, without meeting with any further accident or delay, or "sighting" so much as a "rag" of Wheeler's bobtailed rebs—although the busy-tongued "half-and-halfs" edified us at every station with long yarns about the large force Wheeler had, and their solemn belief he designed to make a simultaneous attack on all the guard-stations upon that particular day—or some other. Well, we guessed it was "some other," for the threatened raid never was made, and we doubt very much if the general ever designed such a foolhardy experiment. Be that as it may, their purpose was to alarm our conductor, and I verily believe they succeeded, as he certainly evinced more nervousness than the occasion seemed to justify. They certainly failed in producing any impression on the furloughed squad, for we consumed the time between Chattanooga and Nashville in laughing, chatting, and that most pleasant of all polite accomplishments, "chawing your friends' terbacker." I might as well add here, we were taught this accomplishment by the ladies of Tennessee. There is no denying the fact—Tennessee ladies are "up to snuff."

In due course of time Nashville was reached. Demands were promptly made upon various institutions of the city, and I am free to confess we found the most of them in *liquidation*, and surrounded by a vast congregation of the patriotic defenders of the nation. They manifested considerable *spirit* in their interest to obtain an interview with the proprietors of the aforesaid institutions.

From Nashville to Louisville our progress was retarded by

the trains from the north being all out of time, and at many
stations we were delayed for some hours awaiting the arrival
of trains then due. It soon became monotonous and tiresome,
and as night approached, individual members of our squad
wrapped themselves in the " mantle of their thoughts" (having no other, and the night *was cool*,) and resigned themselves
to the selfishness of silence. Others, again, manifested their
impatience in the rapidity and voracity with which they mas-
ticated the weed, or the peculiar animus they possessed and
developed in repeated efforts to spit on some sleeping civilian's
polished boots; while all certainly exhibited anything but
pleasure at the slow rate of speed at which the train was
moving.   There was that in the group of half-civilians and
half-soldiers comprising the inmates of the car in which I sat,
which afforded me pleasing reflections, and as I sat and noted
their different attitudes, expressions and hasty, curt ejacula-
tions, I fell into a train of thought, the burthen of which would
if written, prove anything but a compliment to humanity in
general. The "wee sma' hours" crept on apace, and yet I
slept not. A feeling of disquietude, of restlessness, a something
indescribable yet surely felt and almost seen, harassed my mind.
I arose, let down the car window, and looked out upon the
sombre shadows, chasing each other with lightning speed, as
onward moved the train. The very motion of the car annoyed
and irritated my restless spirit, and every cough of the ponder-
ous engine seemed to me to be in rebuke, as it came moaning
and plaining to my ear. I never felt thus before, and I was
half inclined to quarrel with the fancy that next offered itself
in apology: " but then this old, iron-willed monster forgets he
is drawing soldiers—soldiers going home!" Happy suggestion!
giving the key-note to all my restlessness, and fathoming whatever of *omen* I was inclined to regard my feelings as indicating.
Yes, I was going home; going slowly, yet going home; and
thus, thinking of home, I slept.

In the early morn all were aroused by the loud, cheery voice of our conductor:

"Wake up, boys! Louisville—terminus!"

The next moment the squad of discontents were on their feet, and all was life, clamor and confusion.

"Hurrah!" shouted one, "near God's country at last!"

"Bully for God's country!" responded a cavalryman, with an adjunct so expressive of his morality it left a doubt in my mind as to his ever reaching God's country.

"Now for refreshments and substantials!" cried some one, and pell mell out of the car they rushed, joyous and gay as they had been despondent and weary but a few hours before.

Yes, "refreshments and substantials," and they went for them as only a soldier knows how; but, let me tell you, there is quite a distinction in a soldier's view and appreciation of the two—as evident a distinction as exists in the palate of a New York alderman between clams and turtle, or a milk-punch and a glass of lager.

Louisville is notable for three objects, worthy of appreciation and admiration—its beautiful ladies, "*its refreshments*," and George D. Prentice. The last can not exist outside of the smiles and plaudits of the first, and the two named revel in the luxury of the second.

We trod once more the soil of our native State. We felt she had of right just claims to be one of the foremost in the noble band of sisters who stood up boldly in defense of the Union, and we regretted with a sigh the apostacy of many of her leading men, who so ruthlessly divided the feelings of the people, and led them after the gods of Anarchy and Ruin.

From Louisville across the Ohio to New Albany, thence to Mitchell, thence *via* the Ohio and Mississippi Railroad, the squad pursued their journey. Nothing of interest occurred *en route*, and at last we reached St. Louis, at which point we expected to have separated, each pursuing his separate and individual choice homeward. However, upon comparing routes we found that our squad was nearly all going some distance further in the same direction, and we agreed upon the North Missouri R. R. as the nearest and speediest route for all.

In our squad and residents of Iowa, beside myself, were three other soldiers, all of Page county, namely, Barnum, Rose and Mobley. We were also joined in this city by Edward Pace, a discharged soldier, also a resident of Taylor county, Iowa. Some of the Missouri boys being very anxious to get home, left St. Louis on the evening train, September 26th, while the remainder of us concluded to rest over that night in the city and take the morning train for St. Joseph on the 27th. Accordingly a division ensued and quite a number left the evening of the day we arrived in St. Louis. That evening while at the depot of the North Missouri Railroad, I entered into conversation with a gentleman who had come down the road from Macon on that day. He, ascertaining that we were furloughed soldiers and designed to go upon the road, remarked, that he did not consider the Government was doing right in permitting the mail trains to pass over the road unguarded; stating at the same time, that the entire route would soon be infested and controlled by guerriilas; that large bodies of them had been observed for a few days past near Sturgeon, Centralia and other points, and that he felt confident they contemplated an attack soon. He said, also, that the directors of the road had been informed of the fact, but they apparently paid no attention to it. The intelligence thus received, I am confident, was imparted in good faith and with the intent upon the part of the gentleman giving it, to at least place us upon our guard. From occurences that speedily followed, I am satisfied every word he said with reference to the apathy of the directors of the road, was founded in truth—not to admit their apathy originated in no worse design, or complicity with the rebels themselves. Even this latter view of the case has long been honestly believed by many cognizant of the affair, and to me seemingly justified, by the facts I learned from the guerillas afterward. Be that as it may, the intelligence was anything but satisfactory or pleasant to me, and I was greatly concerned in my mind as to the welfare of the boys who had preceded us on the evening train, as I supposed naturally enough the guerillas would attack at night rather than daylight. In this, however, subsequent events proved me mistaken. I soon retired to rest, but I could not sleep. A vague presentiment of impending evil or trouble seemed to burthen my thoughts, and when at last I fell into a slumber it was broken and disturbed by strange fancies of "war's alarms," and again and again the long night through my vision was harassed by such frightful scenes in my dreams. I awoke at an early hour feeling very nervous and very much depressed, and yet not one thought of the danger apprehended seemed to apply to myself, but all my solicitude and anxiety was centered upon my companions. Who can account for this palpable evidence of what was to come, being so clearly detailed to me in dreams?

CHAPTER III.

Adieu to St Louis—The Squad at St. Charles—Aboard the Train —The Warning Unheeded—Near Centralia—Our Conductor—Centralia and the Guerrillas—The Capture of the Train —The Robbery by Wholesale—Ordered into Line—The Massacre in Cold Blood of Union Soldiers!—Saved from Death!! —A Prisoner of the Guerrillas!!!

At a very early hour on the morning of September 27th, 1864, our boys took seats aboard the mail train for St. Joseph, Missouri, and leaving St. Louis in the gray mist of morn—the train ran rapidly up to St. Charles, where crossing the Missouri River, you proceed to Macon, connecting with the H. & St. Jo. R. R.   This was to have been the point where we would have overtaken the boys who passed up the evening before, and you will judge our surprise, when entering the car at St. Charles we found our boys had laid over at this point instead of proceeding on to Macon.   A question or so, soon satisfied us that *they* had heard the same intelligence at St. Charles which reached us at St. Louis, and they *felt* a good deal better and *braver* at the sight of so many boys in blue. There is no use denying it, if not alarmed, they were considerably excited before leaving the city of St. Charles by the common chat of the employes in and about the depot.   From their hints and half uttered warnings, given it is true, in badly uttered and rough language such as the following: "Ye are

brave now ain't you? Begorra an ye need to be, for the guerrillas will be after ye, sure!" Such sallies being only received
by our boys by some similar reply, reflecting upon the courage of the rebels; and yet, one could easily see that too general
a knowledge of the presence of guerrillas upon the road was
present, to doubt or question the truth of the information.
Having once had my suspicions aroused it was a difficult matter for me to allay them, and I watched keenly every movement of our conductor prior to the start of the train. I did
not like the man's countenance, and circumstances which have
transpired since, have left the impression indellibly fixed upon my mind, that in some way, that man was a party to the
Centralia massacre. As though conviction of his participa-
tion in that infamous act yet haunted his imagination, two
years afterward, that same conductor *refused* to "*go out on
his own train*," upon learning that myself and a number of the
comrades of the slain soldiers of Centralia were aboard the
train. Why he acted thus, I am unable to say, as I am not
aware that any threats of danger to himself, had been made
by any of our party in his hearing; yet he positively refused
to go, and another conductor took charge of his train. Perhaps it was as well he took the precaution to remain at home.

At last the bell rang its parting clang of warning. All
aboard our car were in evident excitement, and showed all
that expectant anxiety of expression which marks the soldier's
features upon the eve of battle. There was, strange to say no
gloom or despondency, and I do not remember a day during
our whole trip when the boys appeared filled with brighter
hopes or fonder anticipations. They felt they were nearing
home—they were—that immortal home, prepared for us beyond
the skies! Happily unconscious of the fate that awaited them,
as of old, upon the tented field, they whiled away the time.—
The train sped onward, and as station after station was

reached and passed, no new rumor or intelligence was received to add any fuel to our lately-excited fears.

Onward, yet onward thundered the train, bearing unconsciously in its grim, fierce way its freight of human souls toward eternity!

Hark! the shrill scream of our iron horse give us, again, warning of a station; and with this dying note, a clank and a clang, the train stops—Mexico is reached.

Here all was excitement. Rumor made mountains of mole hills, perhaps, but there is no denying this fact—all said, and *some knew*, guerrillas were on the road. Our conductor made his usual call for "telegrams" at the station office. I was told that he received one from Centralia. Its contents I know not; but this I do know, he was repeatedly notified by civilians at the station that it would be dangerous to pass further up the line without a train-guard. Of course he had a train-guard? Did he not have twenty-seven old soldiers—whose uniforms, alone, would scare off guerrillas? He might possibly have acted on this thought, for he evidently paid no attention whatever, to either information or remonstrance.

Amidst much excitement the train moved forward and many an eye gazed for the last time in life upon each other. It seemed to me, and others, that our train was soon moving at an unusual speed, so much so, indeed, it was made the subject of comment both among civilians and soldiers; and all were hoping it would continue until we passed the threatened danger.

And now, dear reader, as I approach a description of the final horrors of the massacre, my arm grows weak, my sight is dimmed, and my heart sickens with the recollection. To read an account of the affair at the time it transpired, (when the mind of the public, in a sense had become accustomed to

such details of blood,) was, in itself, a task replete with mingled feelings of repugnance and wondering horror at the cruelty
of man to man. How much greater, then, the agony and distress of my mind when (believing myself reserved only for
some more malignant and torturing death,) I stood near the
doomed men, drawn up in line to meet the awful death the
cruelty of their captors awarded them.

But, again to the details, sickening and atrocious as they
are.

Upon the approach of the train to Centralia, it soon became
evident our fears of an attack were not entirely ground-
less. Quite a large body of mounted and dismounted men
could be seen in and around the station buildings, and as we
drew nearer the excitement increased among the boys, as some
of them recognized peculiarities in the crowd that stamped
them guerrillas, and our natural enemies. The train was
moving rapidly, and our hope was based upon the conductor
passing at full speed. Probably from obstructions on the
track, or from reasons of own, he failed to make the
attempt, and sounded the whistle to stop. I was seated beside
a soldier of the First Iowa Cavalry, and when he heard the
whistle he jumped up, looked out of the window, and turning
back to us, said :

" There are guerrillas there, sure !"

In a moment more we were inside a line of blazing, murderous weapons, and volley after volley was poured into the train
until we came to a dead stop. Our fears were active as to our
fate, for we were totally unarmed. Scarcely had the motion
of the train ceased, ere with yells and shouts the guerrillas, in
a body, rushed toward the cars. In a moment after, the door
of the car in which our squad, or a larger number of them sat,
was burst open, and in crowded our grim, fierce captors, shouting " Surrender ! Surrender !"

Our boys had collected about the center of the car, and apparently looked as though they intended resistance to this demand. Some one of the guerrillas continued:

" Surrender quietly, and you shall be treated as prisoners of war."

Some one of the boys answered, " We can only surrender, as we are totally unarmed."

In a moment, changed was the spirit of our conquerers. The olive branch of peace, the protestations of humane treatment were withdrawn, and learning our defenseless condition, these half-cowered wretches of the moment before, became the lawless free-booters, the inhuman monsters, Rumor had always designated them. For each guerrilla to single out his man, threateningly present his weapon and demand the life or money of his powerless victim, was but the work of a moment—an evidently pre-arranged matter, so quickly and quietly was it done. Not one man escaped, so systematic was their plan, and so eager their greed for plunder.

Had we escaped with this, how much of grief and sorrow would loved ones have been spared! The worst, however, was yet to come. When we were ordered to " fall into line," our hearts were filled with vague apprehension of their purpose; and when ordered to strip off our clothes, these suspicions became certainties, and we began to contemplate the king of terrors—death—as perhaps our speediest deliverance from a worse fate. The fatal line was formed. Twenty-seven soldiers—unarmed, defenseless men—were arraigned before this tribunal of demons to expiate by death a crime no worse than loyalty to their native land! History has no parallel to the monstrosity of the conception of the act—much less its execution. But, thank God, honor and loyalty are brave words!—aye, cheering words, even in the hour of death. Men, great men and good, have died for the love of them; but search where you may, in history or in fable, and it will be found difficult to produce a single instance where men prepared for certain death so calmly as those brave men. No emotion, no faltering, no entreaty—only the fixed determination to meet cruelty by sublimity, and in the presence of devils, to die like gods!

The line was formed and ready. Stripped of all save their under-clothing, the men awaited calmly the fatal signal—the last sound that would greet their senses on earth. You may imagine the thoughts occupying their minds—the emotions playing in their breasts. How different all these from the anticipation of yester eve! For a moment now total silence ensued around the doomed men. Faces surrounding us gleamed with devilish hate or complacent scorn. Few, if any, dared manifest even the expression of sympathy upon their features. Anderson, the chief of the guerrillas, approached the line. The squad of executioners awaited only his signal, and for a few seconds the eye of their chieftain wandered thoughtfully over the doomed men. He suddenly addressed them: "Boys, have you a sergeant in your ranks?"

The silence remained unbroken. No one answered from the line. We only wondered what his inquiry would lead to.

Again the chief repeated his inquiry. Silence, solemn as the grave, pervaded the rank. Once more, and in a louder tone, he asked the question; adding, "If there be one, let him step aside."

Almost involuntarily, I moved beyond the rank, still wondering what could be his purpose, and fearing to continue longer silent, as I observed the man who had taken my coat approach his chief, and I knew that the stripes on my sleeve would designate the rank I held.

Anderson then came forward himself, and directed two of his men to take charge of me and remove me from the spot.

They at once conducted me to the rear, and I halted there reserved for what fate I could not then fortell.

There were other men in that doomed line, holding the rank of sergeants, and to this day it has been a matter of wonder to me what impulse compelled me to advance. If they thought as I did, as to what the question of the guerilla chief tended, I can now see and appreciate their object in preserving silence. His object in the selection of a sergeant from that rank, I then thought, was based on a desire to make some special example in his punishment. Hence my silence, until the moment I saw silence would, perhaps, prove only an aggravation of the punishment designed to be inflicted.

I had scarcely stopped at the position assigned me, when a volley from the revolvers of the guerillas in front, a demoniac yell from those surrounding, mingled with cries and moans of pain and distress from my comrades smote upon my ear. I turned, and, God of Heaven, what a sight I beheld!

The line had disappeared. Many of my late comrades lay dead upon the ground; others were groaning in the agony of their wounds, and yet others, wounded and suffering, were making a last struggle for existence in seeking to avoid further injury. One brave man, Sergeant Peters, made a desperate struggle for his life, and succeeded in felling a number of his assailants, and obtaining a temporary respite beneath the station-office. It was fired at once, and finally by force of circumstances alone the fiends succeeded in killing their victim. Such a scene as I witnessed then, it is impossible to describe. The work of death went on, and one by one my brave comrades met their fate—brutally, inhumanly murdered. The flames roared and flashed about this scene of blood, and the dense, black cloud of smoke hung around the spot, as though to hide it from the light of day. The guerillas, with horrid oaths and wild, fierce looks, gloated over the bodies of the slain, or spurned them from their path with brutal violence. Civilians stood trembling by, eager perhaps to express their sympathy for the dead in words and tears, but fear of a like fate forbade,

A party of guerrillas now set fire to the train, and amidst loud shouts and yells, the whistle sounding its own funeral dirge, it was started up the track. The fiends had now reached a state of excitement bordering on insanity, and then followed a scene of turbulence it is in vain to try to describe.

The position in which I stood, to the rear of a line of mounted guerrillas, only enabled me to become a witness of a part of their infernal orgies. The yells and horrid curses of the wretches commingled with the piteous moans of my suffering, wounded comrades, and now and then I could hear the dull thud of the carbine stroke that ended forever the suffering of some prostrate form.

At last it was over—the Carnival of Blood ended!

This scene, so horrible in its details, thank God was but of short duration; occupying, from the arrival of the train to the death of their last victim, scarcely one hour. So occupied had been my senses in the contemplation of the awful death of my comrades, I had not given a thought to myself; and at last, when I saw naught was left upon which they could further eke out their bloody desires, thought came back to self, and I expected every moment to be called forth, and to become, as it were, the last victim upon the hellish altar of Hate, erected by these demons, and reeking with the blood of innocent, defenseless men.

That I escaped, I—*alone*—thank God! Of my peril, you will hear anon.

No language can be found adequate to express my terror and apprehension of what imagination pictured as my fate, so dreadfully had the scene I witnessed operated on my system.

No word had as yet been spoken, by chieftain or guerrilla

2

that warrauted me in indulging in the faintest hope of final escape from death at their hands.

And here in my recital, let me pause for a moment. Fresh in my memory, as though but yesterday's occurrence, looms up that dreadful scene. Again the fatal volley, that cut down in the vigor of life twenty-six of my comrades reverberates in mine ear! and from out the curtain of flame and smoke that lies like a pall above their maimed, bleeding forms, peer the wild fiendish features and brutal eyes of the guerrillas, gloating in savage glee above the dim and fading vision of my comrades. It is no fancy, this. It is no vivid play of my imagination called up for present purpose. No! It is indellibly traced upon my brain. It is one episode in my life past, never, never to be forgotten! And comrades, when life draws to a close, and the Death Angel waits to waft my spirit hence, I will die as I live, bearing with me the remembrance of all your fortitude, all your sufferings!

Ere I leave you there, where bloody and impious deeds were done, where hands of strangers laid the sod above your hearts, I would ask in your name, and in the name of the great army of the republic, of which you formed a part, some fitting testimonial to be placed above your graves by the noble State in whose soil your bodies lie entombed—and whose sons you were.

Spartan lore offers no heroism excelling thine. Her heroes were the defenders of her honor and her soil. Heroes, then, were you in the resolve that separated you from home and all you held dear, to battle for your native land in the hour of her need; heroes again, in the spirit and fortitude displayed in the campaigns of 1862-3; and heroes for all time to come, in the memory and hearts of your comrades in arms, who have read or will read the story of your fall.

Comrades, though cold in death, to your meed shall be our greatest need; and memory shall brighten at the thought of you, so long as life shall last.

CHAPTER IV.

Awaiting in breathless anxiety and suspense the ordeal, I fancied, through which I was doomed to pass, I noted every movement made by the guerrillas with the keenest interest, expecting every moment to hear the guard ordered to bring forth their man. Apparently something was soon to be done, as they had left their victims where they had fallen, and a number had gathered about Anderson, while the majority went in quest of their horses.

Every one who passed me, in the preparations they were making, heaped abuse and curses upon my head, and not unfrequently a carbine or revolver was placed in close proximity thereto, with the threat: "I would like to kill the d——n Yankee"—"Hell-fire is too good for you, you son of a bitch!" and hundreds of such expressions, too obscene and infamous to bear the honor of being printed. Twice, my guard had all they could do to prevent a drunken squad of them from taking me from them, and it was only by a threat upon the part of the guard of calling for Anderson, they desisted in their purpose. Again and again, I was compelled to endure such abuse from the lips or hands of every guerrilla who noticed me. I never once made reply or attempted to resent these insults, as I well knew, and my guard cautioned me, "that they only sought some provocation from me as an *excuse* to Anderson, in case they killed me." This was the first act approaching anything to humanity I had witnessed from a guerrilla that day, and tended to leave me with a less distrustful feeling of my guard. The guerrillas at last began to mount their horses, and Anderson leading, by twos and twos, they fell into line, and marched out from the station. I was placed upon a mule, and a guard of two men rode on either side of me. The maimed bodies of the Union boys lay where they had fallen, and here and there wandering listlessly among the slain you could observe some few civilians, while others stood idly at their doors, or near the depot grounds, gazing, half amazed and wonderingly, on the scene, as though they had not fully yet recovered from the shock of the revolting spectacle they had so recently witnessed.

The guerrillas proceeded in a north-westerly direction, and toward a temporary camp they had established, about two and a half miles from Centralia. When about a half-mile from the latter place, the noise made by an approaching train was heard, and looking toward its direction, we beheld a freight train approaching Centralia from the south. Immediately twenty or thirty guerrillas detached themselves from the main column and dashed rapidly over the prairie, aiming, it seemed, to intercept the train before it reached the station. We continued on to the camp. I was told by the guerrillas, afterward, that they captured the train and burned it on the track near Centralia.

We reached their camp. It was on the edge of the prairie where the brush and timber jutted up from the southwest, and had simply been chosen as a temporary spot for stragglers, scouts, and others to assemble during their operations on that day. Their horses were unsaddled, and picketed out, while the men threw themselves upon the ground, and in a little while the majority were soundly sleeping away the effects of their inebriation and exciting conquest. I tried to follow their example, and courted sleep in the vain hope it would bring me some ease of mind and body. The very uncertainty that hung about my future, I think, brought with the thought far greater torture of spirit than even death inflicts.

I could not obtain the coveted boon, of even momentary forgetfulness, in sleep; and I at last began wondering and speculating on the circumstances that could possibly have made the quiet, calm host who lay slumbering near, the incarnate fiends whose deeds of blood I had but lately witnessed.

So wondering, I looked upon their chief. I observed him closely; for I felt a singular interest in the man whose simple word had snatched me from the jaws of death. My interest was increased by overhearing the following from the lips of two of the guerrillas, who lay partly shaded in the brush, a few steps beyond me :

"I say, Bill, I wonder how in the h—l Anderson has permitted that d—n Yankee to live so long?"

"Dun no," was the reply; "can't say, lest like 'twas a Providence; for 'taint like Old Bill, is 't ?"

No; I thought, it is not like Anderson. It is not in accord with the nature that so mercilessly ordered, and so calmly viewed the death of brave defenseless soldiers. Can yon pale, sad looking man, be this fiend in human shape? It is possible from evidence I can not dispute; and yet, to study that face now in its passive mood, it looks not like one to be feared, for the sad expression of those eyes, indicates a different character than is generally attributed to this notorious guerrilla chief. Mercy may dwell within his heart; and circumstances, whose cruel hand often warps and destroys the best of natures, may have had much to do in making this one man a living exemplification of the couplet—

Man's inhumanity to man
Makes countless thousands mourn.

Perhaps, a brief description of this notorious and successful leader of guerrilla forces, may be of interest; and I shall endeavor to portray him only as he appeared to me on the occasion of which I write. I have seen him at other times, when "Anderson was not himself," and I would not even do *him* the injustice to attempt a description of his appearance then.

His name will ever be cotemporary with the events that transpired in Missouri during the war of the rebellion—not that there was any act of his during his whole career, which in singleness of purpose or nobleness of patriotism, could exceed in the eyes of his friends, "the Grand Massacre of Lincoln Hirelings at Centralia;" nor one, which in the eyes of all honorable and loyal men, could consign him to so deep an infamy!

William T. Anderson, the leader of the most blood-thirsty and inhuman gang of wretches that ever infested Missouri, was a man of about five feet, ten inches in hight; round and compact in form, slender in person, quick and lithe in action as a tiger—whose nature he at times possessed. His complexion naturally was soft and very fair, but had taken a tinge of brown from his exposed manner of life. His face was in no sense attractive or winning, neither was it repulsive. It only left you wondering what manner of man it mirrored to your view. His eye—said to be the index to character—portrayed not his. It was unfathomable. A strange mixture of blue and gray, the opposing colors sustained by opposing forces, in the war he waged. They were cold, unsympathizing and expressionless, never firing in anger or lighting with enthusiasm in battle. I have his own word for it; they were never known to melt in pity, and I was the first man, who wore the federal blue, who had fallen in his power, whose life he had ever spared. His hair was his greatest ornament, and hung in thick, clustering masses about his head and neck; in color, a rich dark brown. His style of dress and clothing were typical of his life and nature, and seemed to blend something of taste, something of roughness, and much that was indicative of his inclinations and pursuits, in its ornament and the fabric of which it was composed.

To be never called "unarmed" was his great pride and care, one would suppose; for, see him when and where you might, a brace or so of revolvers were stuck in his belt.

Such was the personal appearance of this famous chieftain, and I really believe I have done him justice in the description. At least, I honestly aimed to do it.

Todd, Thrailkill, and others of their officers, sat near Anderson upon the ground, in silence; only broken now and then by some direct question, addressed to some one of their number from their chief. I could not hear their remarks; but once, observing Todd tracing a plan or route on a piece of paper, and handing it to Anderson, I judged they were holding a council about their future operations.

From all I could learn from the conversation of those about me, many of whom had now arisen and were standing idly around chatting in groups, the bulk of Anderson's command consisted of deserters from Price's old Army of the Border, renegades from the Paw Paw militia—many of the latter showing guns they had been furnished by the General Government when they had were enrolled as such. Others of the command were men whom, through some act of violence committed by them, had been compelled to fly their homes, and dared not return.

Suddenly the attention of all was aroused and centered upon the figure of a single horseman, approaching at full speed from a north-westerly direction, across the prairie.

"Bill! our scout," said one of my guards quietly, as he noticed I too observed the commotion his advent was creating.

The words had scarcely died upon his lips, ere another horseman came bounding through the low brush on our right, and galloped straight to where Anderson stood.

His intelligence, whatever it was, seemed of importance, and in a moment the guerrillas scattered in search of their horses, and were seen in all directions mounting and forming into squads of ten or twenty. By this time the first horseman observed before the arrival of the one causing such an excitement, had reached the side of Anderson. The chief addressed only two questions to him, when a mounted man left his side, at his order, and rapidly riding to where my guards and I were standing, said:

"Have your prisoner saddle yon gray horse, and mount him, quick, and mark me, if he attempts to escape in the battle, kill him instantly!" In a few moments the horse designated was by my side, and I was seated in the saddle. Strange, I did not think of or shudder at his threat of death to me! There was then, to be a battle! I only thought of this —of the battle. I wondered if God had sent his Avenging Angel thus soon upon the track of the murderers of my comrades? I longed only to behold the line of federal blue dealing retribution to the assassins? I dreaded not the conflict which, perhaps, would bring liberty to me.

I learned subsequently that the scouts had brought intelligence of the approach of a federal force from Sturgeon, of about one hundred and sixty men, under the command of Major Johnson. The regiment to which he belonged I never learned. He had been at Centralia shortly after the guerrillas who destroyed the last train had left, and leaving twenty-five of his command at this place, was now approaching to give the guerrillas battle.

After riding a circuitous route, occupying nearly an hour, the guerrillas seemed to have reached the spot where they purposed awaiting the onset of the federal troops. A halt of ten or fifteen minutes took place here, and men were sent out by Anderson to observe the advance of the federals. They soon reported back. They were nearer than the guerrillas thought and had halted about a half mile beyond and just over the crest of a hill that completely hid them from our view. Detaching Todd and some hundred and twenty-five men, he divided this force; sending Todd with half their number by the left, around the south side of an old field, skirted by brush and scattered timber. The remaining half, led by Thrailkill, marched by the right. Anderson led the center, and was to do all the fighting; the other force simply acting as a decoy to attract Johnson's attention, and were only to join in the affray, in case Anderson did not succeed in routing the federal line.

As yet we had not obtained a view of the federal forces, and our dispositions for attack completed, the guerrillas moved slowly forward to the summit of the hill. My guard and I rode immediately in the rear of Anderson's company. Hope had gradually been growing brighter and brighter. I trusted more to the circumstance of fortunate accident releasing me in the heat of battle, than in any individual efforts of my own. I was fully resolved, however, to embrace at any risk any propitious moment that might offer, promising liberty to me.

Vain hope! vain dream!

As we cleared the top of the hill, and passed through a narrow belt of scattered timber, the federal line burst upon our sight. The cry "charge!" broke shrill and clear from the lips of their leader, and with one, long, wild shout, the guerrillas dashed forward at the full run upon the little line of dismounted federals in the field. At the same moment both Todd and Thrailkill, their men yelling like so many fiends, appeared on either flank.

Vain hope ! vain dream !

I saw at a glance the battle was already won by the guerrillas, and I was not astonished to witness one volley fired, and too hastily fired, by the federals, proving the force of the resistance made. I saw the defeat of my friends was inevitable ; and yet, I must confess, the courage of that mere handful of boys in blue was worthy of emulation. There was no flinching from the onset of the guerrillas ; but they did all they had time to do, before the enemy were upon them. They were surrounded before they could have possibly found time to reload their emptied pieces, and the guerrillas were riding around and in their ranks, firing, and shouting, "surrender ! surrender !"

Yes, they surrendered. Surrendered as we did at Centralia, with assurances of humane treatment. I *felt* the scene approaching would prove but a counterpart of what I had witnessed at the station, and I shut my eyes to prevent the tears from welling forth, in token of my sympathizing fears, as I beheld the guerrillas proceed to disarm, and render defenseless these "prisoners of war." No sooner was this accomplished than Hell was suddenly transferred to earth, and all the fiends of darkness summoned to join the carnival of blood. Centralia, with all its horrors, was eclipsed here in the enormity and infamous conduct of the bloody demons ! No treatment too brutal, no treatment too cruel to satisfy the greed of that hellish crew ; and were it possible for human souls to grow drunk on blood, I trust the idea may offer some palliation for the scenes enacted there—for the bloody, dastardly, cowardly, wanton acts committed upon the living and dead persons of those brave Union boys! Men's heads were severed from their lifeless bodies, exchanged as to bodies, labelled with rough and obscene epitaphs and inscriptions, stuck upon their carbine points, tied to their saddle bows, or sat grinning at each other from the tops of fence stakes and stumps around the scene. God knows, the sight was too horrible for description, and to be very brief, and sum it all in one expression, " The fiends of hell itself could not exceed the spectacle in enormity of conception, or horror and brutality of execution !"

At the beginning of the battle, or rather before the guerrillas had made their appearance on the left flank, a detachment of twenty-five of Johnson's men, mounted, sat holding the horses of the balance of their comrades, who formed the line of battle. No sooner had the yells of the flanking party of guerrillas revealed their proximity, than this squad sought safety in flight. It was the work of a moment only for the guerrillas to enter in hot pursuit; from five to ten men chasing one federal soldier, and away over the prairie, as far as eye could reach, this race for life continued. Such shouting, firing, running and cursing, I suppose was never witnessed before in a battle; and it is said that the race extended, in two cases, to the very limits of the town of Sturgeon. I was told by the guerrillas, they did not think more than two of the twenty-five escaped their murderous weapons, and that about one hundred and twenty men were slain, belonging to Johnson's command, on that memorable occasion. Fairly crazed with their success and the excitement of the battle and slaughter, the guerrillas started in a body for Centralia, to finish, as they said, their glorious victory in the massacre of the escort left by Johnson at that station, with the few wagons belonging to his command. Fortunately some of the soldiers observed them coming, and succeeded in mounting and getting away. Some few, however, were captured and killed. One man having shut himself up in an outhouse, and being also well armed, the guerrillas used their usual duplicity in order to get him out. He was assured by everything sacred that he would not be harmed; he was told Maj. Johnson and his comrades were all prisoners, and that if he came out and gave himself up, he should be treated as they had been.

In the whole parley they only uttered one *truth*, which the poor fellow found to his cost; for, accepting what they said in good faith, he opened the door, and—was shot dead on the spot! They "*treated him as they had his comrades.*" They did not promise falsely in this. They murdered him!

In a little while it was evident many of the guerrillas were again becoming brutally intoxicated, and in one or two instances difficulties occurred between them and some of the citizens of Centralia, which came near proving fatal to the latter.

In one instance, a man's wife was defending her husband from the accusations of complicity with Johnson, made by a guerrilla, when some one offered her some personal indignity. She instantly resented it with a blow, when the inhuman wretches felled her to the ground, like a beast of slaughter, and otherwise maltreated her person.

At last the order was given to return, and the drunken cavalcade made night hideous as they straggled, without order or discipline, back to their camp.

Repeatedly my life was placed in jeopardy by the careless handling of their arms, and I sometimes supposed the act was *not as careless* as I imagined, as, on several occasions, it required the utmost care on the part of my guard to preserve my life, sometimes doing so only by knocking up the barrel of a revolver or carbine, as it was discharged full at my person.

The camp was reached at last, and three hours given for the

rest allotted to man and beast, ere, as their chief announced, we would be called upon to march.

The night was cool. I had neither coat or blanket, and I could not sleep. I lay and watched the silent stars; and watching, and thinking of all that had passed that bloody day, I wept.

CHAPTER V.

The March by Night—Incidents by the Way—A Prisoner—Guerrilla Chit Chat—The Halt—Signals—Nearly Surprised—The Ride for Life—A Drunken Revel.

From the field of slumber, where lay calmly sleeping in all imaginable postures, the fierce, grim men who composed the guerrilla band, there arose on the still air of the night the given signal to mount and march, and in a moment after, the camp was all life and bustle, in the hurry of preparations for our departure.

My guard told me they designed moving in the direction of the Missouri River, but that they would have to move slowly and cautiously, and by night only, for, says he, "The land will be swarming with blue coats by to-morrow eve. Our late fight will only waken up a hornet's nest about our ears." I thought so too, but discreetly remained silent.

Their march was conducted in a manner peculiar to their discipline, yet with much more order and military *empressement* than I had anticipated. It was very dark, and being a stranger to the country, I was not certain as to the course we were moving, and accepted the guard's statement, that it was in a westerly course. I was anxious to retain the points of the compass, as I yet had hopes of escape, and I felt the importance of preserving my exact location at the time of escape, in my memory.

Hardly a word broke the stillness, and the steady tramp, tramp of the horses, with now and then the jingle of a sabre or spur, was all the sounds to be heard. Our march continued in this manner for perhaps an hour, when the sudden stoppage of the rank in advance, and the rapid closing up of the column indicated something suspicious or something wrong ahead.

"Halt!" was the command from their leader, and "halt" it became. The column, scarcely discernable over twenty paces of its length in advance, remained standing motionless and silent as a statue, in the road. Now the distant hoof-tread of horses could be heard, and the next moment a blue rocket shot far up in the sky, and cast a lurid halo momentarily over the scene. Immediately the command was heard from Anderson's own lips, "Signal men, advance!" and three horsemen, leaving the column at so many different points, rode forward to its head.

Again a blue rocket ascended from the spot marked by us as the line of the opposing party. Were they enemies or friends? No one yet knew. Suddenly two large, brilliant balls of flame, one white, one red, shot far up in the air, from the head of our column. Hardly had the flash burst over us ere the signal was answered. Away in the distance, on our right, it rose and came borne upon the still, quiet air, with a wierd, solemn effect. It was simply a perfect counterfeit of the wild, ominous cry of a specis of owl infesting the wood and timbered bluffs along the Missouri valley. It is strangely unearthly and suggestive of everything dreadful and supernatural to the listening ear of one who hears it for the first time, and is a total stranger to its origin.

The signal thus answered seemed satisfactory, and in a few minutes a squad of mounted men was heard advancing rapidly by a road on our right, which intersected our route a few

rods in advance of our column. After a brief conference with
Anderson, this squad passed to our rear by our right flank.
As they were passing near where I sat, one of the guerrillas
shouted to them, inquiring who they **were** and where they
were going.

They replied: "We have got a prisoner, one of Johnson's
men. We had to chase him a long way, and only settled him
after putting six balls in his body."

"Ain't he dead yet?"

"Nary dead. The devil can't kill him; an' seein' as how
he's good stuff, we shall care for him. We were ordered to
carry him to a house *below*, so you see we will *save* him yet."

Further conversation was interrupted by the advance of
the column, and I parted from them, honestly believing they
were taking him back to the scene of the slaughter of his
brave comrades to finish their hellish work, and add torture
to his death, in the sight that would surround him.*

The march was continued, and gradually divested of the
monotonous silence that had marked its beginning. The men
about me began to converse; the topic being scenes through
which personal members of the band had passed during the
past fortnight. The operations of the day before were dis-
cussed in full, and I learned from their remarks that it had
been rather an "extra occasion," both in point of "plunder
and success." I am sorry to be compelled to add here, that I
also heard relations of other occasions, equally as bloody and
inhuman in point of deed and act, as any that were witnessed
at Centralia.

I tried, in repeated conversations and by leading questions,
to ascertain if they operated, as a command, independent of

* I have learned of late that the prisoner referred to above, *was saved*,
and recovered from his wounds, and is now a resident of Jackson Co, Mo.,
or was, some two months ago.—ED.

orders from higher authority, or if they were enrolled in the service of the Confederate States. They were very chary of their replies, and, as if suspecting my motive, I never found the story of any two of them to agree on this point. Some admitted their officers to be in the pay of the Confederate States, and holding their commissions under the seal of the war office at Richmond; while others denied this statement, and asserted that not one of their number was responsible to, or in any way beholden to the authorities at Richmond. So far as men were concerned, I am inclined to regard the latter statement as correct, and that their "pay" consisted in the "stealings and plunder" obtained upon their forays. I think, however, their officers held commissions under the Confederate States, was paid by them, and consequently were individually responsible for the acts and duties of all men operating under their command, whether paid by the Confederate States or not.

The men came and went from the command at pleasure, on the march, and at all times, except when they were marching to or from an expected battle, or the scene of active operations in the field. I was told at these times it was "death" to the man who absented himself, without permission of his chief.

For a long time I was at a loss to determine how Anderson succeeded in governing so well such a collection of wild, turbulent spirits, as during the entire period I remained with them I never witnessed, nor heard of one single act of cruelty upon the part of the leader toward his men. On one occasion, to be narrated hereafter, I beheld a very wanton and foolish act committed by him toward his command, while he was excited by drink, and with this one exception, his intercourse with his men always appeared cordial and pleasant.

The march continued all night long, and as day began to light up the eastern sky, the halt was called. We were in a low piece of ground to the rear of a farm, near some stacks of oats and hay; and as a matter of course, as nearly surrounded by brush as possible, for they nearly always confined their halts and temporary camps to such spots as these. We rested here for a few hours and the horses were fed from the stacks; the men obtained nothing, save what little some few individuals had saved over from yesterday's supply. I got nothing to eat then, nor during that day. We marched a part of the day by the by-roads and through the brush, and about noon halted in the brush to await the friendly cover of darkness. At night we again mounted and pushed from the brush for the more open country. We traveled pretty lively, but in almost total silence, as a scout who had reached us in the afternoon, imparted the intelligence that he learned federal troops had been seen the day before, moving east from Rocheport, and they were perhaps in search of Anderson.

We returned to the broken and brushy land during the march, and about midnight, halted, with orders to rest until daylight. Springing from their jaded horses, which were soon fed from an old cornfield, but a little way off, and picketed out to graze, with their saddles for their pillows, these hardy wretches soon lay in picturesque postures and abandoned ease, courting the embrace of Morpheus. The night was very chilly, or else the absence of coat or blanket gave that feeling to me. I had not tasted a mouthful of food since leaving St. Louis. I was not to say really hungry, but I was weak, the result of the excitement I had lately undergone. I slept but little. My brain was occupied with thoughts of escape. I closely studied the faces of the men who lay around me, judging with whom to deal in case I needed assistance in the attempt. I believed in the maxim of "every man filling a measure;" and I thought *gold* was the measure most likely to fit the greed of those about me. Oh! that I had the boasted secrets of alchemy, in order to turn whatever I desired into gold.

At last the morning came, and with the first dawn of light, I was roused by my guard, and conducted to where Anderson's horse was feeding. I was then directed to curry and saddle him. This was tough and "against my grain," but I went to work with a "blacksmith's" energy, and I gave him such a rubbing and scratching he'll remember as long as he's a horse.

I think I must have pleased Anderson with the job, for as he passed near me an hour or two later, he reined up his horse, and said :

"Well, my old fellow, how do you get along ?"

I replied, "Very well, sir,"

"Well," said he, looking directly in my eye, " You, my man, are the first being whose life I ever spared, who was caught in federal blue !"

" That's so, Colonel," shouted twenty or more of the guer-rillas, as Anderson rode forward.

Presently a tall, fine looking man overtook the rear of the column as it moved out of the brush, and drawing up his horse, he rode leisurely along beside my guard. I felt sure I had never observed him before among them, as he was dressed in the confederate gray and bore some ensignia of rank upon his coat. I was wondering who he could be, when, observing me, he addressed my guard :

" Who is this man ? "

Saluting, they replied simultaneously, "A prisoner"—one of them adding, " Taken, sir, at Centralia."

"I thought you took *no* prisoners, my man ?"

" This *one*, Colonel, by orders, you see."

" Whose orders ?"

" Anderson's—no, only *reserved* by his orders."

" Aha, I understand. Anderson was right," and spurring forward, he left me to any thing but pleasant reflections.

Reserved! — and for what purpose? I racked my brain vainly, and to no purpose, to arrive at a solution. The officer said he "*understood it.*" Perhaps he did; but it was far from affording me any consolation at the time. I did not understand it, and it was a source of much anxiety and trouble to me. I learned some days afterward who this man was, and how he had joined the band without my observing him. He had joined us with the scout the day before, but being then dressed in the common garb of the guerrillas, he had not attracted my attention. He was an officer of Price's army at home on "leave," and had joined Anderson to ensure his greater safety in returning to the Missouri River—thence to his command in Texas.

Brief as had been Anderson's notice of me, it certainly produced a remarkable effect with his men, and tempered somewhat their former harsh treatment of me. I became less the object of their rude threats and jests—less espoinage followed my every motion, and I must confess the conduct of my two guards (Richard Ellington and Him. Litton)·became familiar and kind, to a certain degree; and, probably, to as great an extent as circumstances admitted. They had always favored me, from the hour of my capture.

The march was continued for a distance of about ten or fifteen miles, when another halt was made for the purpose of the men procuring something to eat, and of feeding the horses. We were near a cultivated field, the brush and timber consisting of a grove of about five acres, lying along the side of this farm. For greater security from observation, we had entered this timber and encamped. The horses were all fed, and a squad detailed to go and procure some provisions for the men.

Scarcely twenty minutes had elapsed before this detail came galloping back, helter-skelter, through the brush, yelling aloud :

"The Yankees are coming! The Yankees are coming!"

"Ride as though hell was after you!" shouted another.

Without awaiting orders as was their custom, each guerrilla sprang to his horse and saddle, and in less time than it takes to write it, formed by twos in column, and, led by Anderson, dashed out of the brush into the road, by which we had entered it.

Hope once more rose in my heart, and the conviction of chances offering for speedy release grew strong, as the loud *boom, boom!* of a field-piece was heard, directly in our advance, and a six-pound shell came whizzing over our heads, and burst with a loud crash among the timber, one hundred yards on our right. The guerillas halted for a moment, when another shell, nearly in line with the former, set them in rapid motion. The column moved hastily by the left to the rear, and making a half circle of the line of the timber, emerged from the brush on the opposite side of the farm from that occupied by the federal troops.

They had been, for the moment, badly frightened; but upon emerging from the trap in which they were so nearly caught, and meeting a broad expanse of open prairie before them, with a loud shout of derision they galloped away toward an eminence in the distance. Lo! the God of vengeance is surely on their path, for no sooner do we reach the spot, commanding as it did a view for miles of the undulating landscape, than they thought there were "twenty Richmonds in the field," for the entire country seemed dotted over with squads of federal cavalry. The artillery had unearthed the game, and now the chase began.

At a glance, their bold leader saw, and at once comprehended his peril. With a shout of peculiar character, and interpreted instantly by the guerrillas, Anderson wheeled, and

dashed by the column at full speed to its rear, halting immediately by my side. In a second's time—excepting Anderson
and eight men who remained with him, the entire column was
dashing away over the prairie, in squads of from five to eight
men, and apparently each pursuing a different course to mis-
lead the enemy's pursuit.

This was a trying moment for me. Here, then, was to be
the *end*. I had no possible *hope* of being carried a "*prisoner
through their peril!*" I had been reserved thus far, through
all, only to meet my fate, when love of life grew strong in the
hope of liberty, and that liberty almost in my grasp!

Anderson sat upon his horse, gazing long and intently after
the flying, retreating men, who had formed the strength of his
command; while the few men who remained, cast restless
and impatient glances at their leader, anon, changing their
direction toward myself. I thought *they* only awaited *his word*,
to consign me, a bleeding corse to the other world. I shut
my heart to every emotion, and awaited the signal, It came
at last. But, merciful Heaven ! how very different from what
I anticipated. Anderson turning quickly in his saddle, and
looking straight at me, exclaimed :

"Prisoner, you must *now ride for your life! Boys, we all
must!*"

And away, away, following the lead of their companions,
over the prairie dashed the little squad. Anderson leading
the advance by some ten or fifteen paces. On, on, twice,
during the next hour, avoiding only by the eagle glances and
acute perception of their leader, several detachments of federal cavalry in our route. It was a most exciting ride; and
ever and anon, the sharp rattle of distant musketry proclaimed
that some of the guerrillas were not so fortunate as we in
avoiding an encounter with the foe. For hours, without
drawing rein or in any way checking the speed of our horses,

we rode in retreat. Once about noon, Anderson detached himself from the command, with orders for us to pursue as far as practicable our direction in a given course, and wheeling his horse suddenly to the left rode toward a grove or thicket situated some two miles away. I noted a significant glance pass between the men as he rode away, but it was not made a subject of remark, and I was left in total ignorance as to his purpose. At last the guerrilla who now acted as leader ordered us to draw rein, and give our horses the benefit of a partial rest from their exertions of the past few hours. We had made a wide circuit, and was not approaching the grove toward which Anderson had ridden, about an hour before, but was about to enter a similar piece of brush and timber, nearly one mile south of the former. Suddenly our leader halted and with a quick gesture called our attention to Anderson, who was approaching us at a rapid gait from the grove last mentioned. He was soon by our side, and told us a federal vidette or out-post was established beyond this timber; and his sudden appearance was all that saved us from riding squarely into it. I noticed our leader and Anderson conversing in low tones together, shortly after; and changing our course, we turned and rode in a northern direction. About half-past four o'clock we entered a heavy piece of timber, and after riding some twenty-five minutes, we came upon a camp in which we found some twenty of the guerrillas, who had parted from us that morning. They were some of Todd's men who had a brush with some of the federal cavalry, in which or two of the men were badly wounded. One by one, squad after squad, reached this point, and I was somewhat surprised to observe many of them drunk. Todd was drunk as a lord, and evidently in a bad humor. From the evidences to be noted around, this spot had served them as a camp or general rendezvous for some time past, and rough shelters had been constructed of poles, bark and boughs, presenting a rude but very fitting and perfect attribute of their ways of life. They seemed to possess some sort of a depository or commissary establishment here, and both "grub and whisky" were dispensed, with a very liberal hand.

The consequence might be easily foreseen. By night nearly the whole command, Anderson and Todd included, were drunk even to madness. God help me, I never witnessed so much profanity in the same space of time before, nor since; and it is my earnest desire, I never may again. They whooped, ran, jumped and yelled like so many savages. Once, Anderson, leaping on a horse, rode wildly through the crowd; firing his revolvers indiscriminately, and yelling like one possessed.

I trembled for my own safety. I felt that no man was safe when reason had succumbed to madness, and all the brutal passions of fiends ran riot. My guards however, were true as steel to their trust, and as far as possible, preserved me from demonstrations of violence.

At last, worn out with revelry, one by one the guerrillas sank upon the ground, and were soon buried in the stupor of a drunken sleep.

During the night it rained tremendously. I had lost my hat during the day, had neither coat, blanket nor vest, and with but an *apology* for shirt and breeches, I sat and endured it all. How very perverse is fortune! Here, with nearly all my captors buried in a drunken sleep, from which it would require a blast of Gabriel's trumpet, to awaken them—I needs must have two guards who "*never drank*," to stand between me and this golden opportunity of escape. *Teetotalers* were below par, in my estimation, just then.

CHAPTER VI.

Upon leaving the camp in the wood, those of the guerrillas who had been wounded in the skirmish of the federals and Todd's men, together with the arms captured at Johnson's defeat, were left at this point. I witnessed here a specimen of "guerrilla surgery," as practised by them. One fellow had a very bad gunshot wound in the hand, who, neglecting properly caring for the same, found, to his sorrow, that it would require some severer treatment than he had administered, to effect a cure. In fact, his hand was in an awful condition, swollen dreadfully, while all the parts adjacent to the wound seemed a living mass of putrefaction, overrun with maggots. The only remedy I ever knew applied, was pouring oil of turpentine upon the inflamed mass, and greatly to the surprise of the operator, as well as myself, it cured the patient.

A council of war was held the morning following the night of the drunken revel, and it was therein determined to divide the force into small squads, appointing at the same time, a spot at which to re-assemble, for the purpose of crossing the Missouri River.

3

They seemed to agree that the country was so thoroughly
excited by their acts at Centralia and the fight subsequently,
that no efforts would be spared to procure their capture, and
it would prove very dangerous for so large a body to remain together. They had no artillery and could not expect
to cope successfully with their pursuers in the field, and they
did not look for another opportunity to strike a blow, until
the federal troops were withdrawn. They therefore agreed
to disband, with the previous understanding that on such a
date all the living would re-assemble to again commence their
operations.

A few were ordered to remain in the immediate service of
their chief, as guards, scouts, messengers, and for such other
purpose as he might require. Both Anderson and Todd now
appeared, and their detail also, appareled in federal uniform,
taken probably from the dead bodies of the slain soldiers at
Centralia, and the field that witnessed the inhuman butchery
of Johnson's men.

The camp was left in no regular order, as to time or numbers, but as each squad got ready, they struck out. Anderson,
Todd—with probably twenty men in all, including my guard—
and I, left soon after the close of the council. We traveled
hard all day until near sunset, when a halt was made
close beside an old church. My guards were ordered here to
take me ahead, some distance ahead. I pondered upon this
order for a long time, and thought it boded no good to me, but
I am not aware at this moment that this halt and council
related to me in any manner whatever. I am far more inclined
to the opinion that the old church marked some *secret* depository of the stealings of these free-booters and wholesale robbers.
After a delay of probably half an hour, Anderson and his
men came up, and observing shortly after this some farm-
houses, we were directed to scatter out and procure something

to eat. The house at which we stopped, fortunately for me happened to contain a thorough Union advocate, in the person of the hostess. Learning my position as a prisoner among the guerrillas, and the only one left of all they had captured at Centralia, she opened her sympathetic heart, and under one pretense and another, succeeded in detaining my guerrilla friends until she was satisfied I had eaten and drank all that I prudently ought, considering I had been before nearly half-starved. If this volume should ever reach the eye of this lady, I beg her to accept a thousand heartfelt thanks of gratitu de from the poor soldier, whose miserable condition she once comforted, in the thought he had one friend near him, when all others were his sworn enemies; and one, too, who in her nobleness of heart and generous soul dared incur the displeasure of his foes, in assisting him in his distress. May God reward her for this one christian act.

We all encamped close by this neighborhood, and obtained a good night's rest. I slept tolerably comfortable, as I had on Anderson's old coat, which he gave me when he adopted the federal officer's uniform. I have got this coat yet in my possession, and many of my friends and neighbors have frequently seen it. In the morning, feeling very much refreshed, we once more mounted and pursued our journey. On that morning we passed a short distance from Rocheport, and stopped at a house near the town. Two ladies came out to greet us, and Anderson held a long conversation with them. They evidently imparted some intelligence unexpected, for he called Todd forward, and after a moment's consultation, Todd returned and sent a man to procure a fine looking mare that was feeding in a pasture belonging to the premises. This animal was saddled and bridled in lieu of Anderson's horse, and the guerrilla chief rode him away from the premises as though "all right, title and interest thereunto belonging" were vested in himself.

We proceeded more leisurely this day, traveling but a very few miles before noon, when we again halted at a large farm-house. The woman of the house and an old looking man came out to meet us at the gate. There was much shaking of hands, and all seemed highly pleased to see Anderson and his men. Their reception of me was not so cordial when told who I was. We here met with a recruiting officer belonging to Price's army. Observing the dress of the men, he had taken the guerrillas for federals and hastily secreted himself in the house. The old man went back to the house and soon re-appeared in company with this doughty knight of the Lone Star. He was a Texan, and as we found afterward preferred the service of recruiting to active service in the field. He and Anderson held a long private interview, which resulted in his becoming one of our party. Anderson presented the two young ladies of this family with a handsome shawl each, which he took from a roll of " plunder " in his saddle bags. That night we lay encamped in the brush, and so close to Rocheport, we could witness the burning of a part of the town, which had been fired by a detachment of federal cavalry, who had been temporarily stationed there, and had just returned from participating in the hunt for Anderson. They had orders to abandon the post, and were making prepa-rations to do so by the light of the conflagration. We could distinctly hear their bugles sound the "troop" or "assembly," and watched them eagerly as they formed their column and marched away. This, then, accounted for the slow and cau-tious movements, confined to the cover of by-roads and unfre-quented paths, made by the guerrilla chieftain on that day ; and I have no doubt he was informed of all the proceedings he witnessed as taking place, from the lips of the

at whose house he was so warmly welcomed, hours before
he saw them transpire.

Another day's weary traversing of timbered brakes and
hollows, by-paths and old blind roads, and totally devoid of
incident worth recording, and again, late in the dusky eve, we
reached a miserable log shanty, situated in the timber,
whose sole inhabitant consisted of a most villainous looking,
cadaverous specimen of the *genus homo*—a guerrilla; and the
custodian and keeper of the surplus wealth of the band, inves-
ted in horse flesh. There were a number of splendid horses
said to be the personal property of their chieftain, while many
others, and good ones too, were public property. We camped
here during the night. From the nature of the surface of the
country over which we had passed that day, I began to think
we were approaching the Missouri River, and ere long I was
assured of the fact by hearing the steam whistle sounding in
the distance. I was told it proceeded from the ferry boat at
Boonville on the river. This was welcome news to me, as I
had fully determined to risk attempting an escape so soon as
they undertook the passage of that river. The whistle was
repeated several times, and I observed its direction, and
tried hard to retain it, but a few hours rambling amid the
brush and cross-roads of the country on the following day
completely obliterated all idea of the location of Boonville.

Another short but painful march, and the guerrillas reached
their camp or rendezvous near Maxwell's Mill.

It was a lovely, romantic spot, and both for security, and
as affording the requisites of a healthy and convenient camp
could hardly have had a superior. Water was supplied by
a large and apparently inexhaustible spring, in any quan-
tity, and so cold and pure it did the "burnt coppers" of
the whisky-loving band remarkable service, in aiding to

cool and invigorate their heated and passionate blood after a night's carousal.

It was customary among the guerrillas to pay and to receive daily visits at this point, from the leading and wealthiest citizens of the neighborhood, and not a house that I saw them enter, thereabouts, but these murderers received the homage and attention best befitting angels, at the hands of the owners. This was the point at which they had agreed, upon disbanding, to re-assemble. We, in consequence of this, remained " bush-ranging " some two or three days, awaiting only the " gathering of the clan " before proceeding to " Harkers," where all recruits and the entire force was to meet, and from thence move hastily beyond the river.

Some really laughable and ludicrous scenes occurred between parties of the guerrillas at this camp. On the other hand, it was at times the scene of sore trial and suffering to me. Our squad, and many of the returning guerrillas, wore—either in full or in part—the federal uniform; while others, especially recruits coming in to join the band, were always attired in butternut, or the confederate grey. Frequently these opposing and antagonistic "colors" met accidentally in the woods, upon roads and by-paths; and in several instances "tall running|" for " tall timber " followed, or in others, again, an half-hour's duel ensued; each combatant protected by the interposition of either stump or tree from the fire of his supposed deadly foe. It certainly seemed a difficult matter for these fellows to obtain a proper recognition from the friends of their cause, and many a poor uninitiated " butternut " would endure a fright equal to the pain of his subsequent mortification, when he discovered that his enemy in blue, with whom he had been at deadly feud, was his staunch friend and a sworn supporter of the same principle as himself. During the few days we remained at this camp, I was frequently the object of

marked attention at the hands of these new arrivals. I have
frequently—uncomplainingly and in total silence—undergone
the closest interrogation at their hands, receiving as a reward
the most awful of blasphemous denunciations, while at the
same moment a dozen or more revolvers would be aimed with
all the precision of a photographer's camera when endeavoring
to obtain a *whole* man at a sitting. It is my opinion that a
"dozen whole men" would not have satisfied the inordinate
mania of these villains for practicing "leveling," and if they
were as perfect in the use of the compass, in this respect, they
would have made a capital corps of civil engineers. It was
not at all pleasant to endure, and it is far from pleasing even in
recollection. In short, I witnessed many different phases of
temperament and character, such wide extremes, among the
sum total of their actions, that I should find it almost an impossible task to attempt by any description I might give, to convey
to your mind, dear reader, a just conception of events as they
actually occurred. But of one thing you may rest assured, I,
or they, will perhaps never forget some of the scenes that
transpired in those brief days, when carousal and revelry ruled
the hour, and time was passed in the narration of the most
bloody and horrible events marking the career of each guerrilla
participant. *   *   *   *   *   *   Of these I dare not write.
Suffice it to know that, even now, I would not unveil the
mystery that has buried them in oblivion.

Once more the guerrilla band was prepared for action.
Nearly if not all of the old command had returned, and we
had been joined by many new adherents, with a number of
recruits for Price. From the active preparation I witnessed
being made, I began to fear I should soon be compelled to
again witness scenes similar to the barbarity of Centralia's
awful drama.

The order was at last given for the march, and in the early

morning of October 6th, we all mounted and set out upon a journey, intending as rumor asserted, to ascertain the practicability of a passage of the Missouri River, at or near the town of Rocheport.

On one occasion *en route* we stopped at a large fine mansion, situated handsomely, and surrounded with many evidences that the proprietor was "well-to-do," in the world's way of considering this phrase. Here, a circumstance followed that surprised me not a little. Without any previous understanding on their part, or at least unknown to me if there was, all the guerrillas, my guards included, dismounted, tied their horses and entered the mansion, Anderson ordering me to await their return at the gate of the yard. Here, thought I, is an evidence of unlimited confidence entirely unexpected to me, and I must add also, entirely unappreciated, because I at once divined some devilish motive or design was at the bottom of this singular procedure. I do not think I was altogether mistaken in this, for in a few moments a gentleman, not belonging to the band, but a member of the household probably, emerged from the building and sauntered leisurely across the yard to the spot where I was standing. There was something in his movement that left me with the suspicion he was trying to impress me with the idea that he did not desire the guerrillas to notice his approach to me. It tended to place me upon my guard. He at once entered into conversation, which was in substance about as follows:

"Do you belong to Anderson's or Todd's company, my friend?"

"I am a prisoner, sir."

"What! a prisoner, and left unguarded?"

"As you see—"

"Ah!" he interrupted "then *you* don't think Anderson the bloody, cruel wretch, they would have us all o believe? He certainly shows that he treats his prisoner with much confidence."

"Yes, I have only reason to be thankful. He has spared my life."

After musing a moment, he said:

"These guerrillas, as *they* call themselves, are a careless happy set—they are brave too, and fight well, I suppose?"

I made no answer. He added quickly, "How do you like Anderson?"

"He has treated *me* as well as I could reasonably expect. I have no fault to find."

"You would not like to join his band--you would prefer liberty? Do you know you are near to your friends; the federals are at Fayette, and it is not far from here."

I felt my heart bound. I dared not reply lest my voice would reveal the pleasure I experienced at this intelligence. I had feared we had got entirely beyond the line of federal posts; and that in this fact, the risk of my chances of escape were greatly enhanced. Now I was assured by this man's conversation, that friends were in close proximity to me and I resolved anew, on making a final effort for liberty, when we reached the river.

Some of the guerrillas appearing at the door, the gentleman turned away toward the house. In about fifteen or twenty minutes I was called up to the door of the house, and the ladies (?) of the mansion indulged in some ten minutes' sport, laughing at and deriding my appearance. Before the war I used to think

"That laughing bore no kin to sin,"

and yet, these women, and hosts of other women of the South sinned against the holiest and loveliest attribute of their sex in every smile they indulged, at the expense of defenseless prisoners, or the sufferings of captive foes. I am reminded just here, of denunciation applied to a woman of this character, by a former comrade in arms. "Madam," said he, "*you* look as though your mother's milk had been vinegar, and that you were *weaned* upon the same—*spoiled!*"

Again mounting we started for "Harkers," the point before indicated as the spot of rendezvous for all who designed to cross the river and risk further service under the leadership of Anderson. When a short distance from the house, we suddenly met another party of guerrillas who mistaking us for "feds" fired a volley, but which fortunately harmed no one.

We arrived at Harkers and remained there one day longer than was originally intended, before attempting the passage of the Missouri, a very heavy and violent storm on the night of our arrival having interfered somewhat with the plans of their chief. At Harkers large numbers of the citizens of the country came into our camp, and many and repeated were the gratulations extended between their friends and the guerrillas. Anderson came in for a large share of these attentions, and I too, was somewhat worthy of "note" as I was frequently pointed out as the "*sole survivor*" of all the enemies they had captured. This operated very singularly upon different individuals, and it so powerfully affected the "budding murder" in one youth's heart—a mere boy—he repeatedly begged and petitioned to be allowed to kill the "d——n Yankee."

On the evening of the tenth day of my imprisonment, or rather of my captivity, the guerrillas bade a final adieu to their old stamping-ground and to their confederates at Harkers. Everything was hurry and confusion until the column was in motion, when by express orders, perfect silence was preserved. We rode some six or eight miles and struck

the Missouri river at a point about one mile above Rocheport.
For some reason the spot did not meet Anderson's approval,
and we turned back, passing through Rocheport and again
came to the river some three miles below. The night was
dark, with nothing but star-light to guide a search. I had
made up my mind in the confusion likely to attend their
embarkation, to accept all risks and attempt my escape. I
had everything to gain; only one thing to lose—my life! I
thought of those I loved at home better than my life, and
I was willing to risk the sacrifice of that life, to reach them
once more. You can well imagine then, how closely and
how eagerly I watched every preparation that was being
made. What a jealous eye I kept upon my guard to observe if
possible if any additional restraint was to be applied to me. I
eagerly listened for every word that fell within my hearing to
learn the exact disposition made concerning the manner of
their crossing the stream. I soon learned they had but thir-
teen skiffs, holding say from five to eight men, according to
size. The men only were to occupy these boats—leading and
swimming the horses. By a rough estimate I calculated that
three trips made by the skiffs would transfer them all, and I
was now concerned lest I should fall among the first install-
ment. I was thinking of Fayette and the federal soldiers
there, and had no desire to cross the "rubicon" that would
crush my hopes and defeat my plans.

At last, chance informed me that my guards and I would be
among the last to pass over the stream, and I concluded to
seize the moment of confusion attending their first trip, as the
golden opportunity for the trial I was about to make.

I was soon to take a step attended with eminent peril—a
failure insuring certain death! I was closely surrounded by
many of the most heartless and desperate men the world ever
knew. Yet, I had one, and only one chance in my

favor. It was this: For a day or so back, since, in fact, my conversation with the gentleman, where the guerrillas had left me alone by the yard gate, I observed that I was granted more liberty of action, and had frequently moved about among the men going from spot to spot, without my guards following me or exercising any apparent surveillance over me.

The moment for the trial I had resolved to make, came at last. The men of the command were busily engaged in removing saddles and bridles from their horses, and preparing their lead-halters. The first lot who were to cross were by the boats—the skiff being first occupied by the men, and many of the horses in the water, or about to enter it. All immediately near the river bank were in a state of bustle and much excitement prevailed. Some of the horses proved restive, and the attempt to force them into the water momentarily increased the confusion. At this juncture one of my guards said, "You watch the prisoner, I want to go and see the start," and as he spoke he moved away toward the boats. A moment after, some sudden and increased excitement by the river side attracted the attention of my remaining guard, and he moved about a rod in that direction. I seized the opportunity, and walked rapidly away from the spot, and directly into the crowd of men and horses near me. I passed carelessly through the crowd and emerged near to a dense mass of bushes and brush-wood on the river side. I hastily entered this thicket and walked as rapidly as I could some two hundred yards, and stopped to listen if my absence had been noticed. My breath came fast and my heart beat so rapidly it almost made me faint and sick. I was very much excited. I listened with every nerve of my being strung to its utmost tension, expecting every second to hear the shout of the fiends in hot pursuit. Ten seconds seemed an hour—the time only, I probably paused to ascertain if I had been missed.

Reassured, I hastened forward and was suddenly arrested in my course by distinctly hearing the tramp of horses' feet, and evidently approaching in the direction of myself. I had but just reached an old road, and I hastily drew back into the brush and secreted myself. Four mounted men passed by —guerrillas doubtless, on their way to join Anderson. Thank God, I thought; they were not in search of me! I now paused a few moments, and sought out the North Star as a guide on my course. I walked with all the speed and vigor I possessed, and suddenly emerged from the brush in full view of a house, about the yard of which stood hitched, ready bridled and saddled, some six or seven horses. I was strongly tempted to turn guerrilla for the nonce and appropriate one to my especial use, but I reflected that comfort and ease in this case might not be the best method of insuring safety, so I made a wide detour and passed this spot, without meeting any one from whom I might have obtained some information as to my locality. My earnest desire was to reach Fayette, but I was in absolute ignorance as to the proper direction for me to pursue. It was the only military post I had any knowledge of in the country, and I knew that much depended on how near I was to it, in considering my chances of success in my escape from the guerrillas. Again, I had every reason to believe that Anderson meditated active operations soon, and why not he direct his force against Fayette? I was then anxious to reach the post, and at least place its commander on his guard. I felt very much exhausted; physically, the excitement had proven too much for me, and with slow and wearied step I wandered through the woods until about daybreak, when I entered a road whose beaten way indicated considerable travel upon it. Here was a sign-post, and clambering up to the board at the top, I read by the uncertain light of the early morn the inscription thereon.

I had only traveled, so it informed me, eight miles from the point where I left the river, and yet, doubtless twenty more would not make up the distance traversed by me on that night, so devious and uncertain had been my course. I was very weak and tired, and feeling it would be very injudicious to travel by daylight, I sought me out a shelter wherein I might find rest. Looking about me I observed an old tobacco shed in a field, and I made for it. I found it partly filled with hay, and I crept into it, and making a snug nest, I enjoyed this welcome retreat with all the unctious delight manifested by a grandee in his daily *siesta*.

At night I resumed my journey. I was compelled to travel but slowly because of physical exhaustion from want of food, and the frightful condition of my nervous system. Just about daylight I observed a negro passing near an old field. I hailed him, and he awaited my approach. He told me I was but a mile from Fayette, and not over three or four hundred yards from the line of federal pickets. He pointed out the location of the nearest sentinel to us, and I, thanking him kindly, hastened forward again. This was good news for me—the goal was nearly won! Liberty! Friends! Home! No man, but those who may have had such an experience as mine, can form an adequate or just conception of the emotion then moving my soul. I cried—cried like a child. Strong man as I thought myself, I felt that, in the hands of the Providence that had so far preserved and guided me, I was but as the merest babe!

I paused for a few moments to calm my feelings and collect my senses, before I presented myself before the guard; and when I again advanced, such was my zeal to meet my friends and feel assured of safety, I had almost forgotten that my guerrilla dress would make me an object of suspicion, even to them. I was soon assured of this, however, for at a sudden turn in the road, "Halt, there!" greeted me, and looking up, I

stood face to face, about twenty paces removed from a cavalryman, dressed in the "bonnie blue" of my loved country's
uniform. I instantly halted, awaiting his further challenge.
The formula of "the service" over, the sentinel was convinced
I meant no harm, and allowed me to approach sufficiently near
him, so as to hear my story; and when at last it was received by
him, calling his corporal, the intelligence was instantly dispatched to post headquarters. In about half an hour I was
conducted there in person, and received very kindly by Capt.
Eaton, of the Ninth Cavairy, commanding the post, who
seemed to sympathize deeply with me in the relation of my
sufferings, and he at once dispatched intelligence of my escape
to general headquarters at St Louis. I also communicated
what intelligence I possessed with regard to Anderson's and
Shelby's commands.

The command at the post belonged to the Ninth Missouri
Cavalry. I feel greatly indebted for their generosity and kindness extended to me, and I need no better assurance than their
humane and christian sympathy for the distress of a fellow-
being, to indite here, they were honorable and brave boys in
the field of action. I ever shall remember those boys with the
kindliest of feelings and lasting gratitude. The little garrison
was thrown into an unusual excitement the day following my
arrival, by the sudden advent of a scout with the information
that Shelby and Anderson had united, crossed the river at
Booneville, and designed marching against Fayette. My
account of the horrible affair at Centralia and of Johnson's
unfortunate defeat tended perhaps to increase the excitement
n anticipation of an attack from the perpetrators of such bar-
barities, and for awhile the report of the scout caused the
command undue anxiety. There is one thing, however, that
should be stated here perhaps, and that is, this mere handful

of men—sixty all told—were, to a man, opposed to an evacuation of the post, as was proposed, in case the scout's information should prove correct. It certainly would have been an inexcusable blunder, or an event ending in horrible *murder*, on the part of Capt. Eaton, to have abandoned his post on unreliable information, or to have attempted its defense if assured beyond a doubt that it would be attacked by such an overwhelming force as would leave the "defenders defenseless," and but the victims to guerrilla hatred and outrage. He therefore dispatched a trusty Union man—a citizen—in quest of the desired information.

He returned to us in a very brief time, stating we had barely time to save ourselves, much less any of the few military supplies accumulated at the post. Shelby was said to be within eight hours march, and we were ordered to abandon the place as speedily as possible, and march for Macon City on the St. J. & H. Rail Road. We accomplished this without much delay, and at Macon I bade adieu to all my kind friends of the Ninth. I took the cars here for St Joseph, at which city I gave the editor of one of the papers, a very brief statement of such facts as I have recorded in detail here.

I reached my home in safety. Of what transpired there, I shall not write. You have many of you felt, perhaps, that such meetings as these are sacred to the participants, and not to be held up for the scrutiny of the world. * * * *

To the Almighty Ruler of Heaven and Earth we owe our existence and the blessing of life to day; and though it is a seeming mystery to us why His benificence should single me from the great number slain on that memorable occasion as a living example of the sacredness of His promise in the Word, yet in truth and honor of soul and spirit, to His name and His Providence be all the honor and praise.

To our comrades of the gallant old 25th Regiment, and to

the Boys in Blue of the corps to which the First Missouri Engineers were attached, one word more, ere I bid you adieu. I have endeavored in this little volume to as faithfully perform as my abilities would admit, the oft-repeated promises made to you in years bygone. I have written for you the "story" so often told by the camp-fire, on the picket, and yet again and again, whenever the name of a "fallen comrade" reminded us of the "blank" Centralia's Horrible Massacre" left in our ranks and upon our muster rolls. Have I performed this "duty" well, or poorly, it rests not with me to say—I have only sought to do it truthfully.

Comrades, wherever you are, if this little volume should meet your eye, I ask you to read it, and having done this pay to the Memory of our dead comrades, the tribute of "A Soldier's Tear."

We append here the names and residence of such soldiers as Mr. Goodman was intimately acquainted with, and of whose death he was an eye witness. He regrets his inability to give entire a list of the names of all those who fell at that massacre, but as he was not personally known to any but the following named, he declines to trust his memory in giving other names, regiments or places of residence of any of those with whom he had but slight acquaintance.—Ed.

NAMES.	REGIMENT.	RESIDENCE
Edmund Pace....	First Mo. Eng. Regt...	Taylor co., Iowa.
James Mobley...	First Mo. Eng. Regt...	Page co., Iowa.
Cass Rose.... ...	First Mo. Eng. Regt...	Page co., Iowa.
—— Barnum....	Twenty-Third Io't. Inf	Clarinda, Iowa.
Josiah Comer....	First Mo. Eng. Regt...	Nodaway co., Mo.
Chas Hilterbridle	First Mo. Eng. Regt...	Nodaway co., Mo.
Sergt. Peters.....	First Mo. Eng. Regt...	Holt co., Mo.
James Thomas ..	First Mo. Eng. Regt...	Buchanan co., Mo.

www.ingramcontent.com/pod-product-compliance
Lightning Source LLC
Chambersburg PA
CBHW021515090426

42739CB00007B/625